D1604923

		DATE DUE	

"Each one of my blues is based on some old Negro song of the South.... Something that sticks in my mind, that I hum to myself when I'm not thinking about it. Some old song that is a part of the memories of my childhood and of my race."

—W. C. HANDY

COVER PHOTO

Portrait of W. C. Handy
© Bettmann/Corbis

Published in the United States of America by The Child's World®, Inc.
PO Box 326
Chanhassen, MN 55317-0326
800-599-READ
www.childsworld.com

Product Manager Mary Francis-DeMarois/The Creative Spark
Designer Robert E. Bonaker/Graphic Design & Consulting Co.
Editorial Direction Elizabeth Sirimarco Budd
Contributors Mary Berendes, Red Line Editorial, Katherine Stevenson, Ph.D.

Library of Congress Cataloging-in-Publication Data
Summer, L. S., 1959-
W.C. Handy : founder of the blues / by L.S. Summer.
p. cm.
Includes index.
ISBN 1-56766-927-1 (alk. paper)
1. Handy, W. C. (William Christopher), 1873–1958–Juvenile
literature. 2. Composers–United States–Biography–Juvenile
literature. [1. Handy, W. C. (William Christopher), 1873–1958.
2. Musicians. 3. Composers. 4. African Americans–Biography. 5. Blues
(Music)] I. Title.
ML3930.H27 S86 2001
782.421643'092–dc21

2001001077

Contents

W. C. HANDY IS BEST KNOWN AS THE MUSICIAN WHO MADE THE BLUES POPULAR. HE WAS THE FIRST PERSON TO PUBLISH BLUES SONGS, MAKING IT POSSIBLE FOR MORE MUSIC LOVERS TO HEAR THEM. TODAY PEOPLE ALL OVER THE WORLD ENJOY PLAYING AND LISTENING TO THE BLUES.

A World of Sound

Whoo-oo-rit! Whoo-oo-rit! The shrill sound of a whippoorwill dots the air. Rat-a-tat-tat! A woodpecker adds the drum. The Tennessee River roars in the background. High in the hills above the river, in the town of Florence, Alabama, nature makes music. And music is important to many of the people who live there. One boy growing up in Florence listened closely to the sounds around him. As he grew older, he continued to listen carefully to all kinds of sounds and music. His love for music's rich variety led him to play a new kind of music called the **blues.** The boy was W. C. Handy, known as the "Father of the Blues."

William Christopher (W. C.) Handy was born in Florence on November 16, 1873. His mother, father, and grandparents all had been slaves. One of W. C.'s grandfathers, William Wise Handy, tried to escape slavery through the Underground Railroad. The Underground Railroad was a secret network of people who helped slaves escape. But William Wise Handy was caught and returned to slavery. Still he did not give up. He managed to get an education in secret. When slaves were freed after the **Civil War,** he became a minister in the Methodist Church. He owned property, which was rare for black Americans at the time. He also built Florence's first church for blacks. William Wise Handy was an important and respected man in his community.

Christopher Brewer was W. C.'s other grandfather. Brewer was a slave who was very loyal to his master. Near the end of the Civil War, armed robbers attacked and killed Brewer's owner. They were looking for money the owner had hidden. Although he was beaten and shot, Brewer would not tell the thieves where the money was. Later in his life, W. C. Handy wrote about his two grandfathers in his **autobiography.** He said that he had **inherited** a little bit of both their personalities. He fought for what he believed was fair and right, like William Wise Handy. And like Christopher Brewer, he recognized a person's worth, regardless of race.

W. C.'s father was Charles B. Handy. He was a Methodist minister like his father, William Wise Handy. W. C.'s mother was known to her family as Babe. W. C. also had a younger brother named Charles. The Handy family did not have a lot of money, but they still had a good life. They lived in a simple but comfortable log cabin set in lush woodlands. Food was plentiful, and they never went hungry. Even so, money for extras was hard to come by.

Charles and Babe Handy were religious people. They had a deep appreciation for hymns and **sacred** church music. **Secular** music that was not written for church was a different story. Charles and Babe did not like secular music and did not allow it in their home. But young W. C. loved all kinds of music. His musical talent was clear even when he was a young boy. His grandmother joked that his big ears meant he might be a musician one day. W. C. found ways to listen to as much music as he could. Friends and relatives told him about other types of music. Sometimes they would even play music and let him play along.

W. C. attended the Florence District School for Negroes. He was an excellent student, especially in math. Not surprisingly, he excelled in music. His music teacher at school, Professor Y. A. Wallace, recognized his talent. Professor Wallace became an important person in W. C.'s life. He provided firm guidance in W. C.'s musical training. The school did not have a piano or organ, so the students focused on singing. Everyday objects such as combs, tin pans, and milk pails all became musical instruments. W. C. enjoyed this part of school very much.

But Professor Wallace did not share W. C.'s love for all forms of music. Like W. C.'s parents, Wallace disapproved of secular music. They believed people who played music **professionally** were dishonorable. One day W. C. announced that he wanted to be a musician when he grew up. No one was happy to hear this.

When he was 12 years old, W. C. wanted to play the guitar. He secretly saved the money he earned from odd jobs. Finally, he had saved enough.

Library of Congress

LIKE THE FARM WORKERS SHOWN IN THIS PICTURE, HANDY'S PARENTS
AND GRANDPARENTS HAD ONCE BEEN SLAVES. AFTER THE CIVIL WAR
ENDED SLAVERY IN THE UNITED STATES, THE MEMBERS OF THE HANDY
FAMILY WORKED HARD TO BUILD A BETTER LIFE FOR THEMSELVES.

The thrilling day of W. C.'s purchase ended in heartbreak. When he brought the guitar home, his parents were shocked and disappointed. They made him exchange it for a dictionary. From then on, W. C. kept his plans secret.

Without telling his parents or his teacher, W. C. learned to play the **cornet.** His way of doing this was amazing. A bandleader gave music lessons at the barbershop. W. C. watched the lessons through the window. He learned the fingering patterns and then practiced on his desk at school. Later a musician sold W. C. an old cornet for $1.75. He began to make real music. From then on, W. C. was hooked.

Against his parents' wishes, W. C. began playing with a band. He also sang with a **quartet.** When he was 15 years old, he went on tour with the band. They traveled to other parts of Alabama and to Tennessee. But the bandleader quit and left the band stranded. Before the bandleader left, he gave W. C. enough money to take a train home. The bandleader did not feel right about abandoning such a young boy. But W. C. did not go back to Florence right away. Instead, he split the money with the rest of the group. They toured on their own for a while, often singing for their supper. Eventually they returned to Florence, happy with their adventure.

This trip was W. C.'s first taste of life on the road. It might have been short, but it was sweet! W. C. was not only a gifted musician, he was a natural entertainer. He loved traveling and making music for people.

Corbis

W. C. HANDY BOUGHT HIS FIRST CORNET AS A
YOUNG BOY. HE DIDN'T KNOW IT AT THE TIME,
BUT THIS INSTRUMENT WOULD HELP TO MAKE
HIM A POPULAR PROFESSIONAL MUSICIAN. HE IS
SHOWN HERE IN THE 1930s PLAYING
A TRUMPET BEFORE A LARGE AUDIENCE.

Handy Hits the Road

William C. Handy finished school in 1892. His first job was as a schoolteacher in Birmingham, Alabama. Teaching didn't pay very well, so Handy looked for other work. He took a job at the Howard and Harrison Pipe Works in Bessemer, Alabama. His new job paid $1.85 a day—more than he made as a teacher.

Music was still Handy's first love. He started a brass band in Bessemer and then became the leader of a small string orchestra. Handy taught the musicians how to read music. Because of his knowledge and good manners, he earned the nickname "Professor." Handy became well known and well liked. He enjoyed living in Bessemer.

Many changes were happening through-out the United States. Before the Civil War, most people had lived and worked on farms. By the 1880s, steel, lumber, and other industries were developing. Jobs like Handy's at the Pipe Works were attracting more workers from the farms. Great cities sprang up to house the changing population. There was more money in the country, but this new wealth brought new problems.

The South was much poorer than the North. Race relations had always been difficult in the South, and poverty made things worse. Poor blacks and poor whites were forced to compete for the same jobs. Whites used their power to make things more difficult for blacks. They created laws to keep blacks out of many public places, such as restaurants, trains, and buses. They also made it difficult for blacks to vote.

Hard times came to Bessemer. The Howard and Harrison Pipe Works was forced to cut wages, so Handy went back to Birmingham. But things weren't much better there, so he went to St. Louis. Handy was only 19 at the time. Wherever he went, he became a figure in the local music scene. His gift for music improved every band he joined. Usually he became the leader of the band.

AFTER FINISHING SCHOOL, HANDY LEFT FLORENCE TO WORK AS A TEACHER IN THE CITY OF BIRMINGHAM, SHOWN ABOVE. BUT TEACHING PAID MUCH LESS THAN OTHER JOBS OF THE DAY, SO HANDY DECIDED TO TAKE A JOB AS A LABORER AT HOWARD AND HARRISON PIPE WORKS IN THE TOWN OF BESSEMER.

Handy settled for a time in Evansville, Indiana, and became a member of the Hampton Cornet Band. The band was invited to Henderson, Kentucky, to play at a barbecue. Handy liked Kentucky a lot. He especially liked a young woman who lived there. Her name was Elizabeth V. Price.

Henderson was also home to a German singing group. Handy admired their director, Professor Bach. Handy decided to move to Henderson. He took a job as the janitor at the singing group's performance hall. There he learned by watching, just as he had outside the barbershop years before. He watched Professor Bach closely and listened to all the new sounds around him.

On August 4, 1896, Handy got his first big break. He was invited to join an established **minstrel band,** W. A. Mahara's Minstrels. These musicians were based in Chicago but traveled all over the world. Handy would be able to travel, which he loved. He would also play with some of the top black musicians of that era. Handy was in Chicago just two days later.

HANDY IS SHOWN HERE AT AGE 19, WHEN HE WAS PLAYING IN THE HAMPTON CORNET BAND.

Schomburg Center

Minstrel shows were a popular form of entertainment throughout much of the late 19th century. Some minstrel shows had white performers who used dark makeup to try to look black. The performers also played music similar to that which African Americans played. Many blacks found these shows insulting. But Mahara's Minstrels put on a different kind of show. Although the band's managers were white, all the performers were black. Handy loved this form of music. He felt the minstrel show captured the best qualities of African American music and humor. It also gave black performers a place to show their talent.

MINSTREL BANDS WERE A POPULAR FORM OF ENTERTAINMENT IN THE 19TH CENTURY. OFTEN THESE BANDS WERE MADE UP OF WHITE PEOPLE, LIKE THE MEN SHOWN HERE, WHO WORE BLACK MAKEUP AND PRETENDED TO BE AFRICAN AMERICAN. THIS FORM OF MINSTREL BAND WAS INSULTING TO MANY BLACK PEOPLE.

Handy's talent quickly made its mark on the band. He took on more responsibilities, and his salary grew. Handy used some of his new earnings to buy a C. G. Conn gold-plated trumpet. This was a far cry from his first $1.75 cornet! He practiced on his new trumpet for four to six hours a day. Soon he became a featured **soloist.** His flair for performance attracted lots of attention. The show was so successful, it needed to add a second band. The managers asked Handy to be their new bandleader, in charge of 42 other musicians. Handy enjoyed the life of a performer. He traveled all over the country and had many adventures.

Throughout this time, Handy never forgot the girl he had met in Henderson. On July 19, 1898, he and Elizabeth Price were married. Elizabeth was less than enthusiastic about show business. She would have preferred a more settled life, but she accepted her husband's work. Occasionally, she traveled with the band. It was never easy for her, but she visited places she never would have seen otherwise.

One of the places the Handys traveled to was Havana, Cuba. They enjoyed this trip. The native music of the island moved W. C. Soon after that, he left the minstrel show and the couple returned to Florence. Their first child, Lucile Handy, was born in Florence on June 29, 1900.

Handy immediately set about forming and directing a small orchestra. This group caught the attention of Professor W. H. Councill. Councill was the president of a black college near Huntsville, Alabama. He was also a pioneer among black educators in the southern United States. He invited Handy to oversee all the musical education at the college. Handy, Elizabeth, and young Lucile left for the Agricultural and Mechanical College in September of 1900.

African American music was becoming very popular in America. Cities such as New York and Chicago had elegant nightclubs that featured black performers. **Ragtime,** with its lively, energetic beat, was sweeping the country.

Bettmann/Corbis

WHILE HANDY WAS TRAVELING WITH MAHARA'S MINSTRELS, A NEW KIND OF MUSIC WAS SWEEPING THE COUNTRY—RAGTIME. AMERICANS, BOTH BLACK AND WHITE, LOVED THESE LIVELY TUNES. THE MOST FAMOUS RAGTIME PERFORMER AND COMPOSER WAS SCOTT JOPLIN, SHOWN HERE.

Although ragtime was popular, many formally trained musicians didn't accept it. Handy was among the first to appreciate ragtime. One night at a college concert, he decided to make his point. He led the band in a song called "My Ragtime Baby," but he gave it a different name. The name he chose made it sound like classical music. Everyone loved it—even stuffy Professor Councill!

The popularity of African American music created more work for Mahara's Minstrels. They wanted Handy back and offered him a salary of $50 per week. His teaching salary was only $40 per month. When Professor Councill gave a talk against minstrel bands, Handy made up his mind. He quit his teaching job and returned to life on the road.

Mahara's Minstrels toured in Canada, Mexico, and all across the United States. Some of the places they went were not friendly toward black people. Handy's careful manner and intelligence were as important as his musical talent. His natural leadership helped the band through many tough situations.

But the days of the minstrel show were coming to an end. **Vaudeville** and other new forms of entertainment were appearing on the scene. Radio and motion pictures captured the public's attention. They captured the public's pocketbooks as well, and the audience for live entertainment became smaller.

In 1903, Handy accepted an offer to direct a band in Clarksdale, Mississippi. This turned out to be an important decision. It was the beginning of the road south that led him to the blues.

Bettmann/Corbis

HANDY WAS ONE OF MANY FAMOUS BLACK PERFORMERS WHO ONCE WORKED IN MINSTREL SHOWS. COMEDIANS LIKE THE TWO MEN SHOWN HERE OFTEN GOT THEIR START THIS WAY. BLUES SINGER GERTRUDE "MA" RAINEY PERFORMED WITH MINSTREL BANDS BEFORE SHE BECAME WELL KNOWN. TWO RESPECTED JAZZ MUSICIANS, JELLY ROLL MORTON AND DIZZY GILLESPIE, BOTH PLAYED WITH MINSTREL BANDS AT THE BEGINNING OF THEIR CAREERS.

"Goin' Where the Southern Cross' the Dog"

Handy and his band were very popular. They traveled to cities in many parts of the South. One night, Handy was waiting for a train. The train was delayed for nine hours, and Handy started to doze. A strange sound grabbed his attention. It was a guitar being played in an unusual way. The player was a thin man dressed in rags. He had holes in his shoes. While he strummed, he pressed a knife against the strings along the neck of the guitar. The knife made the guitar's sounds more **flat.** This distinctive sound was the "twang" of the blues guitar.

Handy first noticed the strangeness of the sound. Then he noticed the sadness of the man playing. The man's face told of the sorrow shared by many people in the South. As he played, the man sang "Goin' where the Southern cross' the Dog," repeating the phrase three times. The man's sadness, the strange sound of the guitar, and the odd words struck Handy deeply. He asked the man what it all meant.

The meaning turned out to be quite ordinary. The "Yellow Dog" was a nickname for the "Yazoo Delta" train line. This train ran east and west between Clarksdale and Yazoo City, Mississippi. It crossed the north- and southbound tracks at the Moorhead station. This traveler was going to Moorhead, where the southbound train crossed the track of the "Yellow Dog." He was simply singing a song about it while he waited.

This style of music was an early form of the blues. It had several special features. An important one was the flattened sound made by pressing the knife against the guitar strings. This sound was echoed in the man's singing style. Handy listened closely to the singer's voice. He heard a pattern in the flattened notes. Today these are known as "blue notes." Handy had the amazing ability to identify a sound's notes just by listening. This is called "having a good ear" for music, and Handy had one of the best.

Gail Mooney/CORBIS

HERE B. B. KING, ONE OF THE MOST FAMOUS BLUES MUSICIANS IN THE WORLD, PLAYS HIS GUITAR AT A MUSIC FESTIVAL IN FRANCE. TODAY MANY PEOPLE ENJOY THE DISTINCTIVE SOUND OF BLUES MUSIC—AND THEY HAVE W. C. HANDY TO THANK FOR IT.

Another important feature was that singers would repeat a line two times in a verse. This pattern is also found in the **work songs** that began during slavery. Slaves would sing in the fields as they worked. They were not singing because they were happy. Instead, they sang to express the sorrow in their lives. African American historian and activist W. E. B. Du Bois called these the "Sorrow Songs." This name is similar to the idea expressed in "the blues." One of the reasons the slaves sang was to relieve their aching hearts.

The **rhythm** of a work song was based on the work being done. It matched the pace of planting, harvesting crops, and other hard labor. It was impossible to play an instrument while doing this backbreaking work. Most historians agree that the blues came from the work songs of slaves. **Spirituals** also played a part.

After slavery ended, life changed in many ways for the former slaves. But although the slaves had been "freed," there was really nowhere for them to go. Most remained in the South. The most common form of work for blacks was still field work and other manual labor. Life was still very hard.

The changes in music reflected the changes in the way African Americans lived before and after slavery. The slave traders had brought Africans from many different locations and tribes. The **plantation** work songs were a form of communication between strangers with a common bond. The blues, on the other hand, expressed feelings that were more individual. Singers sang about their personal problems, especially romantic ones. They sang of the sadness of day-to-day life. They were no longer limited to the rhythm of hard labor. They were also free to play musical instruments.

That night at the train station stayed with Handy for a long time. The song began to haunt him. But Handy was a well-trained musician. He valued the formal study of music. He read many books on the laws of sound and the proper ways to write a song. The man who sang "Goin' where the Southern cross' the Dog" knew nothing about that.

Corbis

THE BLUES HAVE A SPECIAL SOUND THAT IS EASY TO
RECOGNIZE. BLUES MUSIC OFTEN HAS A SAD, MOODY
QUALITY THAT REFLECTS THE FEELINGS OF THE SINGER
OR MUSICIAN.

The Burns Archive

Handy was also a professional entertainer. He wanted to make music audiences would like. He wasn't sure they would like the blues. One night in Cleveland, Mississippi, the audience spoke up loud and clear. They asked his band to play some "native music." They wanted to hear something like the song Handy had heard at the train station.

Like Handy, the members of his band were formally trained musicians. They didn't really play the music the audience was asking for. Instead, members of a local black band offered to play. This group had only three members, and they looked scruffy. Their instruments were old and weathered. And by some standards, the musicians really weren't very good. They played the same few lines over and over again.

THE BLUES ORIGINATED FROM THE WORK SONGS THAT SLAVES SANG AS THEY LABORED IN THE FIELDS. THE RHYTHM OF THE MUSIC MATCHED THE PACE OF THE WORK BEING DONE.

The elegant members of Handy's band watched in amazement as the crowd went wild. The audience even threw money on stage for the local band. To Handy, it looked like more money than his band was being paid! Now he was convinced about this new kind of music.

Handy and his band returned to Clarksdale. Handy immediately taught some "native music" to his band. He joined his formal training with what he heard and observed. Handy developed several arrangements based on the blues. One of the first songs was called "Make Me a Pallet on Your Floor." Handy's hugely popular "Atlanta Blues" was another early blues arrangement. Adding this music to their performances was a big success. Handy's band became more popular than ever.

Corbis

THE EARLIEST COUNTRY BLUES MUSICIANS WERE USUALLY SINGERS WHO PLAYED THE GUITAR. THEY OFTEN SANG ABOUT SORROW AND HARD TIMES. TODAY MANY MUSICIANS, LIKE THE MAN SHOWN HERE, STILL ADMIRE THIS COMBINATION OF WORDS AND MUSIC.

The Blues

Once people had only sung the blues in railway stations and on the street. Blues performers were not trained singers and musicians. They did not write and publish their music. But W. C. Handy would change all that. He would bring the heart and soul of the black experience to the attention of people throughout America and all over the world.

In addition to his Clarksdale band, Handy also led a band in Memphis, Tennessee. He traveled to Memphis twice a week. Under Handy's care, this band grew to be one of the best in the South. From dances to store openings, they were in demand!

Many black musicians played in Memphis, and whites began to appreciate their style of music. Black musicians were often hired to "drum up votes" for white politicians. E. H. Crump was running for mayor of Memphis in 1909. His election committee hired Handy's band to play for Crump's campaign. Handy decided to write a special song for the occasion. It was an instrumental number called "Mr. Crump."

Crump won the election. No one really knows if it was Handy's song that did it, but it certainly helped. The song was popular long after the campaign ended. In 1912, Handy decided the song should be published. That way other musicians could buy the sheet music and play the song for their audiences. He changed the title to "The Memphis Blues" and began looking for a publisher.

No blues song had ever been published before. The large music publishers weren't interested. Then a man from the music department of a local store had an idea. He suggested that Handy pay for the printing himself. Another man in the music publishing business got in on the deal. They suggested that Handy pay to have 1,000 copies printed. If those sold well, they would print more.

They call it stormy Monday,

but Tuesday's just as bad.

They call it stormy Monday,

but Tuesday's just as bad.

Wednesday's worse, and

Thursday's oh so sad.

BLUES LYRICS

THE LYRICS OF A SONG ARE THE WORDS THAT ARE SUNG ALONG WITH THE MUSIC. MOST BLUES SONGS HAVE LYRICS, AND THE WAY THEY ARE WRITTEN IS ONE WAY TO RECOGNIZE THIS KIND OF MUSIC. A BLUES SONG USUALLY HAS SEVERAL THREE-LINE STANZAS, OR GROUPS. THE FIRST TWO LINES ARE REPEATED, THEN THE LAST LINE RESPONDS TO THE FIRST TWO, OFTEN WITH A RHYME. MANY BLUES LYRICS ARE SAD, LIKE THESE WORDS FROM THE SONG "STORMY MONDAY," SHOWN ABOVE.

Unfortunately, these men were dishonest. They were familiar with Handy's music and guessed the song would do well. But they wanted to make money for themselves—and keep Handy's share as well. They secretly printed 2,000 copies. Almost half of those sold in just three days. The dishonest men showed Handy the 1,000 copies that remained.

Handy thought those were all of the copies they had printed, so he became discouraged. When the men offered him $50 for the **copyright,** it seemed like a good deal.

OVER THE YEARS, HANDY (STANDING IN FRONT CENTER, ON LEFT) LED MANY BANDS. WHENEVER POSSIBLE, HIS MUSICIANS PLAYED THE BLUES. HANDY WAS PROUD OF AFRICAN AMERICAN MUSIC AND WAS PLEASED TO HAVE THE CHANCE TO SHOW-CASE IT.

Schomburg Center/Layne's Studio

The publisher immediately ordered another 10,000 copies printed. But now Handy had no legal right to the **profits.** As it turned out, "The Memphis Blues" was a big hit. Within six months, the publisher ordered another 10,000 copies. They were sold in cities all over the United States—New York, Denver, Omaha, and of course, Memphis. Sadly, Handy earned no money from these sales.

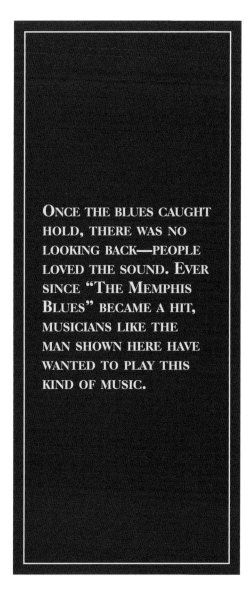

ONCE THE BLUES CAUGHT HOLD, THERE WAS NO LOOKING BACK—PEOPLE LOVED THE SOUND. EVER SINCE "THE MEMPHIS BLUES" BECAME A HIT, MUSICIANS LIKE THE MAN SHOWN HERE HAVE WANTED TO PLAY THIS KIND OF MUSIC.

Mosaic Images/Corbis

Florence Department of Arts and Museums

HANDY IS SHOWN HERE WITH THE MUSIC FOR "ST. LOUIS BLUES," THE SONG FOR WHICH HE IS MOST FAMOUS. SOME PEOPLE CONSIDER IT THE GREATEST BLUES SONG OF ALL TIME.

A Gentleman of the Finest Kind

Handy did not learn the truth about "The Memphis Blues" until 1939 or 1940. But he knew the song was doing very well and that the publisher was making a lot of money from it. He did not give in to bitterness, however. Instead, he vowed to write an even bigger hit.

In fact, he wrote many. Handy was determined to surpass the success of "The Memphis Blues." He and his wife had moved to Memphis. They now had four children, which sometimes made it difficult for the **composer** to concentrate. One night in 1914, Handy left his house without a word. He rented a room on Beale Street and stayed there until he wrote a new song, "The St. Louis Blues." Some people consider this the greatest blues song of all time. Many famous musicians and singers have performed it, including Bessie Smith and Louis Armstrong. It is still popular today. "St. Louis Blues" is a true American classic.

Handy also wrote a song inspired by the traveler at the Clarksdale train station. Eleven years after he heard about "where the Southern cross' the Dog," he wrote "Yellow Dog Blues." Other popular Handy songs include "Aunt Hagar's Blues," "Loveless Love," "Beale Street Blues," and "Hesitating Blues." Handy continued to draw his inspiration from traditional black hymns and folk blues songs. He applied his knowledge of composing to these basic themes and created an entirely new form of music. This form has continued to grow and develop. Many talented artists and musicians love to play Handy's music.

Handy continued to be a successful bandleader and composer throughout his career. He was also in the music publishing business. He and his partner, Harry H. Pace, formed The Pace & Handy Music Company of Memphis.

In 1917, Pace & Handy moved to New York City. The company specialized in black music. Pace & Handy published the songs used on the first blues record. These songs were sung by Mamie Smith, the first black woman to make a record of any kind. Pace & Handy also became the nation's most important music publisher for black composers.

The increasing popularity of the blues brought new competition. Pace left the company to form his own recording business. To make things worse, Handy began to lose his eyesight. He would eventually become blind. Times were hard indeed, but Handy's many friends and contacts came forward to help him. In 1920, he and Harry Pace decided to end their partnership. Handy changed the name of the business to Handy Brothers Music Company, Inc., and rode out the hard times.

In 1926, Handy edited a collection of folk and blues songs. It was called *Blues—An Anthology* and was one of the earliest books of this type. In 1933, Handy wrote his autobiography. He first called it *Fight it Out* but then changed it to *Father of the Blues.* This book was published in 1941. In it Handy told the colorful story of his life as a musician and performer. Handy also shared with the reader his **philosophy** of life. The pages are filled with his humor, compassion, wisdom, and intelligence. In 1938, he published *W. C. Handy's Collection of Negro Spirituals,* a collection of the African American songs he so admired.

In his later years, Handy lived out his legacy as the father of the blues. He held concerts highlighting the development of the blues. He was featured on the first program of a radio show called the "Negro Achievement Hour." He gave talks and lectures across the country about the blues and African American music.

Schomburg Center

IN THE 1940s AND 1950s, HANDY'S HEALTH KEPT HIM FROM PERFORMING AS OFTEN AS HE WOULD HAVE LIKED. BUT HE STILL TOOK THE STAGE WHENEVER HE COULD. HE IS SHOWN HERE IN 1943 PLAYING THE TRUMPET BEFORE AN AUDIENCE OF AFRICAN AMERICAN SERVICEMEN AND THEIR DATES.

William Christopher Handy died on March 28, 1958, but his influence in the world of music remains strong. There are many tributes to his greatness. W. C. Handy Park in Memphis and the W. C. Handy Museum in Florence stand in his memory. The most important award in the blues music industry is named for him. B. B. King, Bobby "Blue" Bland, Koko Taylor, and Luther Allison have all received the W. C. Handy Blues Award. In 1995, Eric Clapton won the W. C. Handy Award for Special Achievement. And every year, Handy's hometown of Florence honors him with the W. C. Handy Music Festival.

Perhaps Handy's memory lives on most clearly in his songs. The words and music take us back to a time gone by, yet the feelings they express are timeless. Handy told the story of ordinary people. He expressed it with character, compassion, and genuine understanding. W. C. Handy listened to the calls of the birds and the rush of the river. He listened to the songs of pain others pretended not hear. In doing so, he heard the heartbeat of us all.

W. C. HANDY DIED IN 1958 AT THE AGE OF 84. HIS CONTRIBUTION TO THE WORLD OF MUSIC REMAINS IMPORTANT TODAY AS BLUES MUSICIANS PERFORM FOR HUGE AUDIENCES ALL OVER THE WORLD.

The Bettmann Archive/CORBIS

Courtesy of the W. C. Music Festival/Mark Baggs

TODAY BLUES MUSICIANS TRAVEL TO HANDY'S HOMETOWN OF FLORENCE TO PERFORM IN THE W. C. HANDY MUSIC FESTIVAL. THIS CELEBRATION HONORS HANDY'S DEDICATION TO MAKING AFRICAN AMERICAN MUSIC A POPULAR ART FORM. HERE SINGER DIHANNE BROWN-WESTFIELD PERFORMS AT THE W. C. HANDY HOME AND MUSEUM.

Timeline

1873	William Christopher "W. C." Handy is born on November 16 in Florence, Alabama.
1885	Handy secretly saves money to buy a guitar even though his parents discourage his interest in secular music. When he brings it home, his parents make him trade it for a dictionary. He later learns to play the cornet by watching a local music teacher.
1888	At age 15, Handy tours with his first band.
1892	Handy graduates from school and accepts a teaching job in Birmingham, Alabama. He later takes a job at the Howard and Harrison Pipe Works, earning $1.85 a day.
1893	When jobs become scarce in the South, Handy moves to Missouri and then Indiana looking for work.
1896	Handy joins W. A. Mahara's Minstrels, a band based in Chicago. After the first season, the managers ask him to lead a second group of 42 musicians.
1898	Handy marries Elizabeth Price on July 19, in Henderson, Kentucky.
1903	Handy leaves Mahara's Minstrels and moves to Clarksdale, Mississippi. There he directs a band. While traveling, he overhears a musician playing a guitar in an unusual way. This experience inspires Handy to mix black folk music into his compositions and band arrangements.
1909	Handy writes "Mr. Crump," a campaign song for E. H. Crump who is running for mayor of Memphis, Tennessee.
1912	Handy's "Mr. Crump" is published as "The Memphis Blues." It is the first blues song to be published.
1914	Handy writes "St. Louis Blues."
1917	Handy moves to New York City to run Pace & Handy Music Company.
1925	Handy is interviewed by Edward Abbe Niles about the history of the blues. These interviews become the basis for a book called *Blues—An Anthology,* published in 1926.
1938	*W. C. Handy's Collection of Negro Spirituals* is published by Handy Bothers Music Company.
1941	Handy's autobiography, *Father of the Blues,* is published.
1958	W. C. Handy dies on March 28.
1980	The Blues Foundation establishes the W. C. Handy Awards. They are the highest honor in the blues industry.

Glossary

autobiography (ah-toh-by-OG-ruh-fee)
An autobiography is an account or story of the writer's own life. W. C. Handy's autobiography is called *Father of the Blues.*

blues (BLOOZ)
The blues is a slow, sad kind of music that developed from the songs of African slaves in America. W. C. Handy is called the "Father of the Blues."

Civil War (SIV-il WAR)
A civil war is a war between opposing groups of people within the same country. The U.S. Civil War was fought between the Northern and the Southern states from 1861 to 1865.

composer (kom-POH-zer)
A composer is a person who writes songs or other works of music. W. C. Handy was a composer of the blues.

copyright (KOP-ee-rite)
A copyright is the right to publish and sell an artistic work such as a song or a book. After Handy sold the copyright to "The Memphis Blues," he no longer earned the money from its sales.

cornet (kor-NET)
A cornet is a wind instrument that is like a small trumpet. Handy learned to play the cornet without telling his parents or his music teacher.

flat (FLAT)
In music, a flat sound is lower than the correct pitch (pitch describes how high or low a sound is). A flat sound is a characteristic of the blues.

inherit (in-HAYR-it)
To inherit something is to get it from one's parents or other earlier relatives. Handy said he had inherited the personalities of both his grandfathers.

minstrel band (MIN-strel BAND)
Minstrel bands were popular music groups from the mid-1800s through the early 20th century. Minstrel bands were very theatrical and often included variety acts as part of their shows.

philosophy (fih-LOSS-uh-fee)
A philosophy is a way of living and looking at things. In his autobiography, Handy shared his philosophy of life.

plantation (plan-TAY-shun)
A plantation is a large farm that grows warm-weather crops such as cotton, rubber, and coffee. Years ago, slaves were forced to work on plantations, and they often sang songs as they worked.

professionally (pruh-FESH-un-ull-ee)
To do something professionally is to earn a living at it. Handy's music teacher, Professor Wallace, thought that people who played music professionally were dishonorable.

profits (PROF-its)
In business, a profit is the money that is left over after all expenses are paid. Handy signed away his rights to the profits from "The Memphis Blues."

quartet (kwor-TET)
A quartet is a group of four singers or players who perform together. As a young boy, Handy sang in a quartet.

Glossary

ragtime (RAG-time)
Ragtime is a type of music made popular in the late 19th century. Ragtime music has a strong melody combined with an irregular beat.

rhythm (RITH-um)
Rhythm is the pace or timing of music. The rhythm of a work song was based on the work a person did while singing it.

sacred (SAY-kred)
If something is sacred, it is dedicated to God or to something holy. Sacred music is written for church and prayer.

secular (SEH-kyoo-ler)
If something is secular, it is not religious. Secular music is written for entertainment rather than for church or prayer.

soloist (SOH-loh-ist)
A soloist is a person who performs a piece of music alone. Handy practiced the trumpet so hard that he was soon a soloist for his band.

spirituals (SPEER-ih-chewlz)
Spirituals are religious songs that originated among African Americans in the southern United States. Most historians agree that the blues came from the spirituals and work songs of slaves.

vaudeville (VAHD-vill)
Vaudeville was a popular form of live entertainment in the early 20th century. Vaudeville shows included a variety of performers such as comedians, dancers, trained animals, and acrobats.

work songs (WORK SONGZ)
Work songs were sung by laborers planting crops or doing other forms of hard labor. The blues grew out of work songs sung by African American slaves.

Index

Further Information

Books and Magazines

Elmer, Howard. *Blues: Its Birth and Growth* (The Library of African American Arts and Culture). New York: The Rosen Publishing Group, 1999.

Hughes, Langston. *The First Book of Jazz.* Hopewell, NJ: Ecco Press, 1995.

Silverman, Jerry. *Traditional Black Music: The Blues.* Philadelphia: Chelsea House Publications, 1994.

Web Sites

Learn more about African influences in the development of American music, listen to music samples, and find related links:
http://www.gse.uci.edu/Lessons/blues.html

Get information about the annual W. C. Handy Blues & Barbecue Festival in Henderson, Kentucky:
http://www.handyblues.org/

Learn more about famous American blues artists:
http://www.blueflamecafe.com

Visit the Blues Foundation, an organization dedicated to the preservation of the blues:
http://www.blues.org

Audio

Louis Armstrong Plays W. C. Handy. Columbia Great Jazz Composers Series. Sony Music Entertainment, 1977. This album features Handy's best-known works.